THE RADIO

LEONTIA FLYNN

THE RADIO

WAKE FOREST UNIVERSITY PRESS

WAKE FOREST UNIVERSITY PRESS

Post Office Box 7333

Winston-Salem, NC 27109

wfupress.wfu.edu

wfupress@wfu.edu

ISBN 978-1-930630-84-0
Library of Congress Control Number: 2017953965

Designed and typeset by Quemadura

Publication of this book was generously
supported by the Boyle Family Fund.

*. . . there is a music of words which is beyond
speech; it is an enduring echo of we know
not what in the past and in the abyss*

EDWARD THOMAS

CONTENTS

The Child, the Family . . .

. . . and the Outside World

*Poems Conceived as Dialogues
between Two Antagonistic Voices*

First Dialogue

Second Dialogue

Third Dialogue

Notes & Acknowledgements

The Child, the Family . . .

IN THE BEGINNING

When we had learned that Darwin wrapped his trunk
in ice-cold towels, that Coleridge's inflamed
humours would slink about his drug-racked form,
we were, like, 'woah'. Our bullshit was reframed
as cogent suffering, and a martyrdom,
noble and true, took shape, extending from
the maladies that lately harrow us
—who're bloated, cramped, hungover, migrainous—
back through the Mists of Time to some first cause:
a kind of lady-spider's bridge-line spun
out from some far-off, not-remembered room
that splits and divides to hold as it unwinds

*   the spectre of our fragile human flesh*
trembling on the tensed webs of our minds.

3

YELLOW LULLABY

My mother wore a yellow dress ...
—Louis MacNeice

A spill of sunlight and a yellow dress.

A yolk.
A yellow flower.
A candle flame.

A moth-light, moon-like, in the nursery's darkness ...

Every time my daughter cried, I came
barreling out like some semi-deranged
trainee barista: friendly but perplexed,
and in the dark of night, Lo! I was there,
perplexed—and ratty—when she cried again.

And thereafter on each new occasion that she cried:

the *form*, the limb that moved, the light that shone,
the hand that soothed her and the flesh that fed.

The voice-that-wasn't-silence that replied,
there in the night—so she was not alone.

Not talking, I mean, with the unborn and the dead.

ALZHEIMER'S VILLANELLE

The human brain is a web of a hundred billion neurons, maybe as many as two hundred billion, with trillions of axons and dendrites exchanging quadrillions of messages by way of at least fifty different chemical transmitters. The organ with which we observe and make sense of the universe is, by a comfortable margin, the most complex object we know of in that universe.

And yet it is also a lump of meat ... I wish he'd had a heart attack instead.

—Jonathan Franzen, 'My Father's Brain', *How to be Alone*

'I wish he'd had a heart attack instead',
Jonathan Franzen wrote about his father,
of the slow, quick-slow disease that left him dead.

'After they fished his brain out of his head
post-mortem, weighed and chopped it up like liver,
I wish he'd had a heart attack instead;

I wish he'd *stopped at once*. The doctors read
the small, clear signs (that little tissue sliver ...)
of the slow, quick-slow disease that left him dead.'

Imagine a train delayed ... delayed ... delayed
that pulls up without passenger or driver.
I wish he'd had a heart attack instead

of *that* spectacle: our efforts round the bed
to cheer—like some incongruous *bon viveurs*—
off the slow, quick-slow disease that left him dead.

But did we? Had *my* father's 'soul' quite fled?
I cannot say for sure—though no believer—
I wish he'd had a heart attack instead
of the slow-start disease that left him dead.

THE BRUNTIES: AN ELEGY

Let's not have any more poems on the Brontës.
No, none of the weird sisters toiling in the gloom
to fan some inner flame (a grim, *al dente*
gruel might cool nearby), no lamp, no tomb-
like interior filled with—what?—moor-wide minds;
and the father, kind and peculiar: let him drop.
The son too, lone and lost—and all that doom,
cod as their umlaut . . . reboot. Photoshop

in particular the grating nonchalance
with which each contrived of some retro malaise,
quite without warning, to be—presto!—dead
inside an hour, as Emily watched dance
the cherry tree, the Autumn sun's low rays . . .
and 'Alright. Get the doctor now,' she said.

POEM IN PRAISE OF
HYSTERICAL MEN AND WOMEN

Of course only those who have a personality and emotions . . .
—T. S. Eliot, 'Tradition and the Individual Talent'

The world is born of hysterical men and women.
Our teeth are shiny as accidental stars.
The hot, brilliant workings of our firmaments
of protons, atoms, axons, dendrites—laws
unto themselves—sees Hydrogen's slow pull
and bloom collide with giddy helium.
This is our ferment: the combustible
and ferret-like—the itch, the twitch, the squirm
and fault-line, down the soul, out of which springs,
in little children lying in their beds,
impulsive, freaky, dire imaginings.

        And out of the meat and fireworks of the mind
the fuse set there that races to its end.

And the urge, oh yeah, to escape all these things.

BOBBY FISCHER:
VERY DISPLACED ELEGY

After the 1972 24-game match in Reykjavik, Fischer 'didn't play any of the great tournaments, and refused lucrative offers to endorse products saying he couldn't because he didn't use them'.
—Wikipedia

Endgame—the King is toppled. Bobby Fischer,
whose Cold War bout in coldest Reykjavik
gripped the split world, is dead. The game is over.
Rook, Pawns, Bishop plays Knight, Pawns and Rook—
Checkmate.
        High-octane mother: check. *Strain*: check.
(When begged to play by arch-fiend Kissinger
The Soviets suspected dirty tricks:
'Please check the light fittings, yes? Check the radiator.')
Then exile and paranoia: check—I'd take
the snow-cold path to ancient Thingvellir
and trace his short biog there in white and black
from Brooklyn to beard, baths . . . and kidney failure,
through squares solved and unsolved—to understand
the games, these moves, that fix the fitful mind.

I

At the mention of Gerard Manley Hopkins, my mild-
    mannered father
—tender, abstracted—would exercise the right
to revert to type. That is to say: devout; that is,
    proscriptive. He would rather
we did not so bandy the good Jesuit's name about
in talk of '*gay* this' and '*gay* that'—just as he would rather
my sister did not, from the library, request 'sick' *Lolita*.
Like pantomime sailors—yo ho—we roll our eyes.
Somebody snaps on the poisonous gas-fire heater
—and I put off a year or two the hypothesis
I'll form, with a wave, to provoke him to these wobblers
that all in such matters swing from pole to pole;
as Hopkins was wont (his muse being bi[nsey] po[p]lar[s])
to swing from joy's heights, alas, to the abyss
and for whom the mind had 'mountains; cliffs of fall'.

'O the mind, mind has mountains; cliffs of fall
Frightful, sheer, no-man-fathomed. Hold them cheap
May who ne'er hung there . . .' Who's not known the hell
that fashions itself from the third night without sleep,
the third or the fourth, in whose black margins crawl
shrill horrors, and where breathless, pole-axed, pinned
—as though in the teeth of an outrageous gale—
the mind, sick, preys upon the stricken mind.
And 'worst, there is none'—no none—than this wild grief:
Citalopram-wired. Our sweating selves self-cursed.
Oh, 'Mary mother of us, where is your relief',
as Hopkins wrote—but, far gone, at its worst
it's her *first form* I want. Please stroke my hair.
It's alright now. I'm here, I'm here. There, there.

THE RADIO

The radio hoots and mutters, hoots and mutters
out of the dark, each morning of my childhood.
A kind of plaintive, reedy, oboe note—
Deadlock . . . it mutters, *firearms* . . . *Warrenpoint*;
Just before two this morning . . . *talks between* . . .

and through its aperture, the outside world
comes streaming, like a magic lantern show,
into our bewildered solitude.
Unrest . . . it hoots now *both sides* . . . *sources say* . . .
My mother stands, like a sentinel, by the sink.

*

I should probably tell you more about my mother:
sixth child of twelve surviving—'escapee'
from the half-ignited *powder keg* of Belfast;
from its *escalation*, its *tensions ratcheting*
its *fear of reprisals*, and its *tit-for-tat*.

She is small, freaked out, pragmatic, vigilant;
she's high-pitched and steely—like, in human form,
the RKO transmitter tower, glimpsed
just before films on Sunday afternoons,
where we loaf on poufs, or wet bank holidays.

Or perhaps a strangely tiny lightning rod
snatching the high and wild and worrying words
out of the air, then running them to ground.
My mother sighs and glances from the sink
at her five small children. *How* does she have five kids?

＊

Since my mother fell on the Wheel of Motherhood
—that drags her, gasping, out of bed each dawn
bound to its form—she's had to rally back.
She wrangles her youngsters into one bright room
and tries to resist their centripetal force

as she tries to resist the harrowing radio,
its *Diplock* . . . and *burned out* . . . and *Disappeared*.
So high, obscure and far from neighbouring farms
is the marvellous bungalow my father built,
birdsong and dog-barks ricochet for miles;

and wisely my mother plans to hole up here
soothed by the rhythms of a *culchie* life—
birdsong in chimneys, hissing coal-truck brakes—
while women back home are queuing round the block
for their *'Valium, thank you, doctor, Librium'*.

＊

So daily the radio drops its explosive news
and daily my mother turns to field the blow.
The words fall down, a little neutral now,
onto the stone-cold, cold, stone kitchen floor.
Our boiler slowly digests its anthracite

and somewhere outside, in the navy dark,
my father tends to his herd of unlikely cows.
A *Charolais*, the colour of cement,
thought to be lost for days has just turned up
simply standing—*ta da!*—in front of a concrete wall.

My mother, I think, is like that *Charolais* cow
in the Ulster of 1970 . . . 80 . . . what?
with its *tensions* . . . and its *local sympathies*.
She gets her head down, hidden in plain view,
and keeps us close. *'Look: Nothing to see here—right?'*

*

But when the night has rolled round again,
my mother will lie unsleeping in her bed.
She'll lie unsleeping in that bungalow bed
and if a car slows on the bend behind the house,
she's up, alert—fearing the worst, which is:

that a child of hers might die. Or lose an eye.
Or a child *anywhere* die or lose an eye.
That the car which slows on the bend behind the house
—*Midnight* . . . she thinks now . . . *random* . . . *father of five*—
is the agent of vile sectarian attack.

By the top field's wall, our unfenced slurry pit,
(villain of Public Information Films)
widens and gulps beneath the brittle stars.
My mother too thinks the worst, then gulps it back,
and in this way discovers equilibrium.

*

Death in the slurry pit, death beside the kerb.
Death on the doorstep, bright-eyed, breathing hard.
My mother folds the tender, wobbling limbs
and outsized heads of her infants into herself;
she curls up, foetal, over our foetal forms.

Since my mother sailed down the Mekong river at nightfall
to the Heart of Darkness that is motherhood,
her mind's been an assemblage of wounds.
She thinks about Gerard McKinney, Jean McConville.
Later the eyes of Madeleine McCann

will level their gaze from every pleading poster
and pierce her heart like a rapier—needle-thin
as the high, intensely imagined cries of children.
Men of Violence . . . says the radio.
My mother nods, then finally falls asleep.

*

In one version, after my mother falls asleep
the radio's hoots and notes of high alarm
get loose from the cork-lined casket of her head.
They flap like bats. They fuck with the carriage clock.
They settle on her Hummel figurines.

Until the whole structure of that homemade house
strains at its fabric, bulges at the seams
with the failure *not* to hear the radio
—*forgive me, doctor, this is hypothesis,
it's conjecture, really, of the weakest kind*—

and even today, beneath our super-smart
transactions and our tight commercial smiles
(half-heard, regretful, at low frequency)
at the centre of amazed concentric circles,
the radio plays behind an unmarked door.

*

Or sometimes, rather, lying in my bed
I seemed to hear the sound of the radio
issuing from a room, deep in the house.
It told, in mournful tones, how two young men
were *taken from their car beside the road* . . .

and afterwards . . . nothing. All the stars came out
like sparkling glitter in a magic globe
that ends beyond the dunes fringing the fields—
and because I was just a child and understood
nothing at all, I simply fell asleep.

LISTENING TO MY MOTHER
LISTEN TO THE RADIO

The Word The World The Word The World The Word The World The Word
The Word The World The Word The World The Word The World The Word
The Word The World The Word The World The Word The World The Word
The Word The World The Word The World The Word The World The Word
The Word The World The Word The World The Word The World The Word
The Word The World   The Word The World
The Word The World   The Word The World
The Word The World   The World   The Word The World
The Word The World   The Word The World
The Word The World   The Word The World
The Word The World The Word The World The Word The World The Word
The Word The World The Word The World The Word The World The Word
The Word The World The Word The World The Word The World The Word
The Word The World The Word The World The Word The World The Word
The Word The World The Word The World The Word The World The Word

THE RADIO

In a spill of sunlight by the kitchen sink
my mother is listening to the radio.
Foster and Allen are singing 'A Bunch of Thyme'.
Oh such a lovely song, she thinks—she lifts
through the sun-barred window square, and flies away

to be whisked about the sky for an interlude
of indeterminate length, then set back down
as though on a spit or promontory of land.
The Lone and Level Sands—to either side—
stretch far away, and this is Forgetfulness.

What spoor or trails, pathways or paling posts
my father traced—alas—have been erased
and each of his footprints fills, again, with brine.
He must remember . . . to make a mental note
to replace the notes he wrote . . . and then mislaid

but my mother, he's certain, is a force for good,
if a little brisk—a little '*Get Out of my WAY*'—
clattering towards him with the tea.
And her children, grown, who lounge about the house,
they also consider my mother a force for good:

that former urgent Lilliputian tribe
who swarmed about her—importuning love!—
have quit their attentions, suddenly, and strolled off
like bullies bored, and lean and loaf about
sullenly misremembering babyhood.

My mother sighs extravagantly at the sink
and builds in her fancy, stone by impossible stone,
such a Taj Mahal or Tower to her work:
yes, haul it out of the earth's guts in one day,
she thinks, O Lord—then fuck it into the sea.

. . . and the Outside World

Summer is fading when we get the news.
Another rain-soaked, work-stretched, child-struck summer
pulled into bits; one eye's to Syria's
bombing, debated with the Commons' answer,
another's on the progress of my daughter,
who's five now, at the college swimming pool
—quite the improbable and wriggling swimmer,
quick as a slippery fish—but that's forgotten
just seconds later when the moment's still
surface is smashed. We're rocked from top to bottom.

Two texts. I get an email on my phone.
Twitter erupts, it seems, in shards of verse.
Phrases from 'Postscript' serve to set the tone
(under 140 characters),
then struggling to the coffee-shop downstairs
we stand like cattle, dumbly looking on
for something on the widescreen's coverage, where
news breaking here at length, at length it's *said*
after all those reports—online, diverse
and instantaneous—the short word: dead.

It's timely, in a way, to hear from sources
far-flung and disparate, that you, whose voice
made itself heard above your fellow voices

in poetry that leaned in awfully close
to living speech, and which was crafty, yes,
patrician sometimes too, but down to earth,
adept and fluent, all self-consciousness
and forward-motion—oh, and *amorous*
. . . that you should *die*. The media holds its breath.
Then the reaction, which is clamorous.

As all of us, it seems, both men and makers
get to our keyboard to express the loss,
for blog post/status update/evening papers
of everything that you had been to us
who was, if not synonymous with 'verse'
then weather system, backdrop, Northern star,
and moral compass of such bending force
—like it or not—we overlooked just how
you were required as man and mortal source
(not merely 'touchstone', as required here now).

And while our networked culture makes lament
perhaps we're mourning too a passing age:
the Derry homesteads, flax-dams, bagged cement
and benediction—and the *pen*, the *page*,
enshrined in those broadcasts, long-wave, analogue,
in which we watch you, awkward and intent,
declaiming poetry about the bog,
wild-haired, wide-collared, for the BBC—
those I miss too, or what they represent
watching them now . . . a lost *Authority*?

Or is it life more *communal*—that order
your work displayed, its faint whiff of the classroom?
The bag behind the chair, the patient reader
sat with his fellows and content to listen,
while this day shows we favour conversation
from every quarter—now!—hyper-kinetic
and self-renewed—all excess and sensation—
with commentary and meme, so to and fro
we zigzag digitally, thrilled, frenetic
but slowly forgetting how we might go *slow*.

Or slow enough to let the matter settle;
for some small thought to grow before it's *said*—
typed, rather, on the message boards for battle—
there to be liked, disliked, the thing agreed . . .
Oh brave new world: crowd-sourced and quantified!
Of rave reviews, conglomerated hype
for audiences vast, readily-made,
but never mind the minor—or the freelance.
And never mind the few who rarely 'like'
(*loving* intensely), or the witty silence.

And as foretold, our standard is the dollar;
spurred by the age's itchy self-promotion
—our only term of value now 'best-seller'—
'Me! Me!' we cry out, jostling for attention.
'Dumped down' unfiltered, 'written with intention'
you would have called these efforts—unenthralled
by daydream, born both *from* our fragmentation,

toward it (both ignored and over-rated) . . .
which is to say our poetry's installed
with AirCon, Wifi AND is central-heated.

. . . But this is *my* idiom. Not hawthorn stick
or hobnail boot and waxing operatic
about how Lit-Crit culture's getting sick
will only make me seem a touch arthritic
if not potentially undemocratic . . .
So let me row back—boys and girls don't scorn me
for I too bend before the times Mathematic
and Algorithmic; also, pass the tissues,
please understand where I am on my *journey*:
a messed-up woman poet with daddy issues.

'The way we're living, timorous or bold,'
you wrote of Lowell, 'will have been our life';
and all these gripes aside, *I've* not rebelled
but drifted: campus-bound, prosaic, *staff*—
so have no moral stick to beat her with
the Goddess Dullness squatting on our pages
—her language slack, her mind a monolith—
and would it make a difference if I tried
mounting the lectern, auguring Dark Ages?
Me, not just *timorous*, but *terrified*.

The way we're living *will have been* our life:
that steely line—that Future Perfect—cast

in an impending retrospective light
our present efforts, not as some rough draft,
but, mid the multi-platform din and drift,
as instrument and something to get *right*;
which is another thing you will have left
(or *have* left—past tense now—those choices made).
An ethics, which instructs:

Now shut up. Write
for joy. Be deliberate and unafraid.

FIELD OF YELLOW FLOWERS WITH
AIRPLANE AND STANDING FIGURE:
POEM FOR GAVIN TURNING 40

Your *pointillist* oil painting of yellow oilseed rape
under a runway sky, took shape
all through that cataclysmic summer.
This photograph shows us bug-eyed, leaner
—stunned by the usual cocktail
of youth: synaptic, chemical—
and also, in truth, a little androgynous.
Your high-up studio bedroom was a tree-house
perched above dubious, parental ground.
We fled there daily, braced against the wind.

Your studio bedroom, or by some old demesne
wall in Seaford or in Castlewellan;
our picture-postcard South Down days all passed
in a haze of lust—
while at night you parked by harbour walls, intent
on the bulbous, crippling, virtually all-grass joints
rolled by a *really* anti-smoking friend.
Such beauty spots! I felt my mind expand
to a symphony of moonscapes, lilac skies . . .
then one by one my little boats capsize.

We were that old story: we were madly in love,
(We might have been locked up, or married off
in another age) and, of course, totally doomed.
At the point where the domed
sky—a bell jar—swept down to the sea
my Raptures had contracted chronically
to a tight, high *thrum* of terror
and somewhere out there on the burnished mirror
were the disappearing heels of Icarus.
Love, what became of us

who weren't the worst, with uniform bobbed hair,
twin slouches; who could like cropped heather,
walks, rain-dappled lakes
as well as AR90 audio tapes
and the whimsical tones of bands based in the Catskills?
Sometimes I almost hear it still
under the white fuzz (constant, virtual,
diffuse) of daily *meh*—like the radio signal
left on some old transmitter, blindly sending and re-sending:
the faint persistent hum of the first Real Thing.

POEM FOR RUTH IN THE
HEATWAVE SUMMER OF 1995

A windowsill of scavenged antique glass
in green and orange, the concrete 'mezzanine'
of that vinyl-smothered, spoiled Victorian house
in which you kept a dark but spacious flat
sweltered all summer.
Belfast, whose whiff of old atrocity
still hung like sulphur low over its sky,
now found a kind of continental glamour
in fire-escapes that roasted in the heat
and swept to the rubbishy cool of alleyways.
I loved how dust and torpor of the days
stored in the close-packed buildings of the street,
and the siren-sounds that threaded across town.

And you, with your vibe of deviant romance,
were a breath of something better than fresh air.
You were anorexic, scornful, had red hair
and slept on a futon like a baking tray
in a room that smelled of Oxfam and old smoke.
All of which faintly, thrillingly, implied
that people might not really work or breed
but lounge about and draw the dole instead
then drink past oblivion, deep into the night—
like figureheads on an abandoned ship . . . !
So our evenings were an abstract, desert shimmer

receding to a point far out of sight,
we sped towards; a black but welcoming mirror

through which we've passed and dropped from the world's
    edge
to wind up in the science-fiction joke
of 20 . . . 20-*what?* You: bruised, flat-broke,
nursing, at once, a compound hangover
and the grievous slight of being . . . *somehow . . . forty?*
Here in this unexpected, shiny future
two decades of that insecurity
to which your *Que Sera, Sera* gave way
have worn your mood and manners all threadbare
as charity-shop finds: the nylon, lace
and not-sure-what you draped about the place
like magic bunting. Look, what did *we* care:

church bells were banging blandly from the road,
past noon, before we crept out of our pits
for value tea and roll-up cigarettes
—that wholly reliable, unholy cure—
with Sunday paper that we barely read,
still seasick from the voyage home again.
So when my misty eye strains past the screen
it's back to the bombsite of that living room
to watch dust swirl there, like the Milky Way,
in yellowy light from a remembered sun
—because, love, though in quite cosmic disarray
there neither of our fates are written down.

OUT

'Out' we would call it: we are going 'out'—
and the word was a kind of optimistic vapour
hung over evenings, redolent of light,
smoke, 'the encounter with a stranger
in Urban Space'

                              or in Belfast, some friend's friend . . .

'Out' was the clenched drive racing to the end
of every frothy, feminine half-sentence:
a missile aimed at ending difference
like an arrow tensed and sprung—arced out of sight
with this drink's end, and this, and this and this
—as the lamps went out and a bouncer shouted OUT—
like a ball whacked out of bounds and lost in moonlight . . .

The opposite of simply sitting about
in your head, like an egg in eggshell. That was 'Out'.

BUDDLEIA: POEM IN MEMORY
OF ROBERTA GRAY

When we sat in the rickety, improvised
'roof-garden' of your house in Inchicore
we could see over the backyards, to the east
behind the terrace, a sea of buddleia.
It sprouted from bricked-up shops and the masonry
of a tapering adjacent alleyway.

I admired your precocious property-ownership,
your mismatched tea-sets and rococo style
while not knowing you particularly well.
The redemptive future, waiting like a ship
somewhere beyond the city wharfs that day
—with kids and small failures—would afterwards sail away

and leave you high and dry: our roof-top host
forever smiling and pouring out the tea
in a wreath of buddleia. The flower you'd insist
—though nodding and sashaying beguilingly—
was a *weed*, in fact, invasive, and of note
for its deeply destructive and tenacious root.

BLACK MOULD AND MILDEW:
OBSESSIVE-COMPULSIVE
POEM FOR LAWRENCE

You'd propped an apologetic-bossy note
like a greeting card on a florist-shop bouquet:
'Don't touch this. Sorry' under the pilot light
of the kitchen boiler. Around it, disarray,
decay in fact, blooming confusion
in that leased flat I could hardly call my own.

How did it come to this: black mould and damp?
A private life that teetered on the brink,
like Belfast, of devolving back to swamp?
Here was the drama—of the kitchen-sink
variety—in which I played my role
these *twelve years since*: gothic, millennial.

Wet-rot and mildew; how did it come to this?
As the suicide year of 1999
plunged to its end, my mind was a bit of chipped glass
whittling down to seven improbable stone
a look I'd managed to accessorise
with raw dermatological distress.

Which fretful flaying came on the coat-tail
of whatever thing it was at once got loose

to rear and buck, like a live electric cable
with me in tow, later in adolescence—
though about whose ups and downs I was super-discreet
so as not to alarm. Set on my feet

another time, in Edinburgh, worn out,
my candle was so scorched at either end
I was half smoky air—but not in doubt,
when you called to the flat to see a friend,
of what you tried to keep under the radar:
some sort of love affair with soap and water,

a laundry-list of purging ritual
round whose imperative, I learned, you fit
your university lab-work up the hill
and the psychology post-doctorate
which gave you some little insight on your plight.
You were afraid of chewing gum and snot

and for this I'd blame your absent Commodore father
(his inside information on Faslane
and HMNB Clyde let him know as blether
our mutually-cherished Four Minute Nuclear Warning
and comfort you—at *six*—that, truly, instead
you'd be exterminated in your bed).

Cue comic dysfunction. Pills. Sunshine on Leith.
Whiskey with breakfast—and that species of de-mob

happiness, like Snow Days, that comes with
blithely temporarily giving up
on the whole debilitating masquerade
of early and unscripted adulthood.

And as our sybaritic one-night stand
spilled into months—you swabbing down the deck,
me, steering my storm-tossed ship to harbour—and
stricken, I bolted, and you followed back
to gritty and less picturesque Belfast
each night's performance should have been our last,

but each day we once again resumed the steps—
you, like some antic, bearded Fred Astaire
twirling your sponge and rinsing round the taps;
me on the upswing, poised between despair
and vast amusement—in the vivid dance:
of our semi-ironic co-dependence.

What we required in these days was no less
than an eternal, stereophonic present
immured from time: replete and frictionless
with all the outside's *sturm und drang*—that wasn't
yet streaming and all-pervasive—kept at bay
obsessively, for love and poetry;

for love and terror and . . . computer code.
You in your geeky thrall to quaint A.I.

wrote software, open-sourced and modified—
all one-point-O, now, hopelessly passé
your Red Hat Linux days, like the MP3-
player a friend called 'revolutionary'

but cutting-edge back then. Each afternoon,
working at separate desks, a pale, calm light
—after the sun tipped past the attics—shone
onto the freaky guest house up the street
(*swingers perhaps?* we mused) . . . but at my back
I'd hear the floorboards strain and plaster crack

with blue mould and mildew, rising damp and rot . . .
'Don't TOUCH THIS'. When, with slow indifference,
the world crept in, we'd both disintegrate
under a wave—as bin-bags, bottles, cans,
clothing and cash all seethed with 'contamination',
for not *all the water in the wide, green ocean*

. . . is water under the bridge, of course. This crazy
quasi-confessional, in black and white
(coded *my* way now), seems kamikaze
nose-dive, in part, part gap-year anecdote
and I wish you well. We were half out of our minds
and young and smart. We should have been better friends.

FLIGHTS

Excess and melodrama. Constant flight.
If I could have lived continually
between the take-off—from the tarmacked strip
still hyper-accelerated but at bay,
an em-dash set evasively in place,
between one *ad hoc* quarter and the next—
then maybe everything would have turned out alright,
before our bumpy landings, cramped and sour,
and the 'dying light over the dinner plates';
or if, somehow, we could have stowed away,
a screwball duo, tucked under a tarp,
between the ship's launch and its anchorage:
watching the scenes shift, all ozone and brine,
all cortisol-clear along the razor's edge.

POEM ABOUT ALL THE SPACE
I TOLD MY HUSBAND I NEEDED

TAKING BLOOD

The duty nurse is taking a sample of blood
one bright March morning, in a room filled with leaf-shadow.
The stiff, rough polyester front
of her nurse's dress is a shield against my qualms
as she draws the liquid up through a clear, curly tube
away from the pin—like a cork from a bottle top—
then siphons it into one-two-three small vials
which she holds up to the light with a little shake,
a clarety, jewel-coloured *bottoms up!*
twirling the bowl until the tannins drop.

Behind the nurse's back, a tree outside
has coughed its froth of blossoms up the branch.
Astonished, tentative, I thank the nurse,
roll down my shirtsleeve over the sleeve of skin
then step back into the limits of myself
like a marble held on a lattice-work of straws,
and leave the nurse—who tilts the glass again
as if to show me, really, it is half-*full*.

THE FISH IN THE BERLIN AQUARIUM

We had come to the Berlin Aquarium
in the dead of winter—the Tiergarten snow-cold
and monochromatic, some slanted, alpine light
turning a few of the upper windows gold.
Inside, in the dream-like corridors
we press towards the vivid turquoise tanks
to see the grouper and Napoleon fish.
They drift serenely from synthetic banks.

Out of the wrecks of history, small domes
and moulded caves—such ersatz shrunken worlds—
the fish drift up, placid: one then two.
They are large and fantastic as marine balloons,
and have oddly upholstered-looking pearly heads,
the surgeonfish and the gigantic wrasse
staring with rimmed eyes, blank, beyond our eyes.
We move our fingers over the cool glass

as though to tap into their element
which is clear and pale, blue and perpetual
like some outrageous Scandinavian dusk
framed and airbrushed. The fish are hyper-real,
high-definition almost, in this space
and lift their bladder-shapes through watery air
working the fleshy trap-doors of their mouths.
Each moves its mouth, perpetually, in prayer

and seems to be mouthing 'I am, I am, I am'
at intervals. We wonder what they know,
performing their status unselfconsciously
—organically, intent—and if this slow
mime of their movements just beyond the glass
makes them, really, beacons of bright calm,
beyond the faces they present for us,
or mutely harrowed in their comfort zone.

WIVES IN MID-TWENTIETH CENTURY AMERICAN FICTION

I

The greasy starlings that came clattering down
onto the scrub-grown elderberry tree
beyond the baby's mat, and made her cry
have all flown off. The baby's mat is gone

and the child herself—crawled off and taken root—
now skips back in, astonishingly six:
all of our energies and our mistakes
coiled in her limbs, hard graft's unequalled fruit.

II

What does it mean to hear 'now change your life'
and falter, or not to be able to obey
so split in two—then turning, day by day,
inward and downward, thwarted, like the wife

in some grim post-war thing by Richard Yates:
April or Sarah—Ariel in the pine—
salving her stunted self with spite or gin?
Yeah, part of us pities and part shares their fates.

III

Poetry is bullshit egotism:
the trite romance of waking up alone,
gradually, in a room where sun
falls on a chair, a bed, four walls—a prism

of—spare me please!—'essential solitude'
that holds some dumb thought till it clarifies.
Pressed on all sides by urgent needs, sharp cries
(*Iced* drinks are melting!), I am clear as mud.

IV

Now that the elbows-in and head-down grind
of those first years slows, ready to abate
and 'later' that we looked to proves *too* late,
a high, Æolian, melodramatic wind

bangs and disturbs the timbers of the house.
The ornamental cat, meant to bring luck
shrinks on the shelf, its pieces all unstuck,
its mechanism discontinuous.

GIVE IT UP, MORON

after Catullus 8

Give it up, moron: forget it all, let it go.
Chalk up among your losses what's lost now for good.
Once, every day's fierce sun blazed madly for you
when, hot on her heels, you'd scuttle off after *her*
—the girl that you loved, like *nobody* has been loved;
to where, back then—oh yes—it was all fun and games
to do what you wanted, which she didn't *not* want
much . . . so each day's sun blazed in a shiny blue sky.
Now she's said 'no' for real, accept it; don't fight it.
Don't chase after shadows. Don't dwell on your crappy life
but make up your mind to endure this—ride it out!
Do you see—Goodbye! Goodbye!—how I'm riding this out,
sweetheart? This stiff upper lip? And you'll be sorry
when I don't come scampering after you again,
and nobody does, and no one calls you gorgeous . . .
You heartless cow. Let me wish you appalling luck
in future affairs: Who'll love you? Who'll you love back?
And who'll get to kiss you—God!—whose lips you'll bite . . .
while, make no mistake, I'll *do this*! I'll ride it out . . .

GOVERNMENT SERVANTS

after Catullus 28

Government servants with your dinky backpacks,
cohorts of bullshit, at its beck and call:
friend-of-my-youth, and you, my bosom buddy,
how is it going? Have you had your fill
of corporate wine and state-subsidised hunger,
fiddled expenses, claim forms and books cooked
to show some profit? Ah, well I remember,
back in my time, I also cooked the books
for a boss—who then proceeded to bend me down
and slowly, and systematically, fuck me over,
while being, simultaneously, in turn,
yes, thoroughly shafted by *his* manager . . .
an even bigger cock. God help us all
taught thus to aspire to the 'professional' classes:
what blots on humanity. May they rot in hell.

I CAN'T SAY I LOVE YOU

after Catullus 11

I can't say I love you more than, like, my kidneys
S—, you old joker. If you weren't so *good*
I'd hate you the way I hate—well—everyone.
But nothing I ever did or said to you
earned me the death-by-a-hundred-shitty-poets,
courtesy of the FIEND you represented
who sent you, first, this tome of frauds and fakers.
If though, as I suspect, this Awesome Intro
came as a gift from S— the writing tutor
well then, I'm not put out: it's right and good
—and payback for you slacking in the courtroom.
Sweet Jesus, what an awful fucking book though.
That you, with *forensic malice*, sent me on
(knowing, of course, in every likelihood
I'd die of it) . . . a warm bank holiday!
Hilarious! But—no—I'll get you back
when at first light, I gallop into town
and hit the bookshops there: McThing, O'What
and F—Ha! Ha!—I'll gather all the poison
to send *chez vous* by way of counter-torture!
Meanwhile, limp back, you anti-masterpieces—
homeward on the feet you haven't learned to use!
Vermin! Our Age's New Poetic Voices!

ODE TO MOY PARK

(Poem by Keith O'Keefe, the Northern Irish Laureate for Business)

Oh Moy Park, supplier of own-label and customer-
  branded poultry, your contribution to my life, and lives
  of all in Northern Ireland, is far from paltry.
Not only do you produce the large variety of chicken prod-
  ucts I so greatly enjoy
but, also almost 7,000 people, in different capacities, you
  do train and employ
in France and The Netherlands as well as in and around
  Craigavon, which is your headquarters and major man-
  ufacturing site (and let us not be havin'
the usual guff about Craigavon being a failed artificial city
  and industrial black hole
for it is a cheerful and pleasant location on the whole).
Nor, Moy Park, are you confined in your largesse
to the processing of drumsticks, breaded nuggets, buffalo
  wings, battered chicken burgers,
diced tikka pieces, chicken dippers and various other
  portions
available in healthy wholemeal or bespoke spicy coatings.
No!—for your inroads in food-service have also paid
  dividends
in the form of a range of products for our vegetarian
  friends:

battered mushrooms, vegetable tempura and breaded
  camembert!
(Oh when I was a boy, such foodstuffs should have been
  rare!)
At night, over the roads, your great freezer trucks roll,
as, also abroad at night goes my poetic soul—
not filled with frozen chicken, true, but with honest words
  destined as wholesome nutrition
for readers' hungry ears (though in my case, sadly, for less
  remuneration!).
Oh Moy Park, you are apparently owned by a huge Multi-
  national based in Brazil
but, to me, you are our own local boy-made-good still.
The watchwords of your Managing Director, Nigel Dun-
  lop, are 'Being Best by Being Better'
which confuses the comparative and superlative, but to me
  that is of no matter
for Moy Park (and here I am not referring to the anthem
adapted from a popular Tina Turner song, by other local
  groups whose name I shall not mention)
for Moy Park, Northern Ireland's largest food-processing
  company, you are simply the best.
You are simply the best, and (especially since you acquired
  O'Kane Poultry) better than all the rest.

POEM IN HOMAGE TO BUILT
THINGS IN THREE DIMENSIONS

Sunlight, yellow, on an upright gable
standing by waste-ground, a bright autumn sky
behind it and a foreground of low rubble,
transforms place into geometry —

the nice arrangement of adjoining planes,
almost like a work by Malevich.
Here are the big quotation marks of cranes.
Train tracks. Tramlines. Suddenly a bridge

staked out, foot by foot, over the river
—form as a virtue of necessity:
tensed suspension cable, cantilever,
and canyon. I like these relics of industry.

I like warehouses too: the heartfelt views
from high loft windows onto square, grey yards;
old balconied apartments in Cadiz
in cobbled streets; marble; misericords

under the seats of medieval churches,
bombed to just the naves—their empty shells
deep and rectangular like lidless boxes;
anywhere weed grows on windowsills

or structure finds its guarded heart exposed—
for we shall give up what's interior
(a townhouse on our route that has been razed
except two corner walls, frayed wallpaper);

or mills slumped by canals; the struts and stilts
of factories rusting back to skeletons;
in broken-open cupolas and vaults:
gudgeons, anchors, hoopings, stays and chains;

for all of this we're pleased to see convert,
to something else, in a bright heaven where
held on the open network or closed circuit
our brilliant concourses are light and air,

with building blocks and freight of one and nought;
for wagon after wagon of fast goods
—experience itself, perhaps, pure thought
or pure potential . . . Icons? Wingless birds

flitting with ease across limitless space
—all that is instant and intangible;
transparent bills hung on an interface
transparent too—so on that gable wall

where some forgotten manufacturing sign,
'Take Courage', say (*try*, even if you don't)
remains in place, we smile to see sun shine
on crumbling brickwork and on faded paint.

MALONE HOARD

In coffeeshops on the Lisburn Road we eat with mobile phones beside our plates: our shiny black talismans. Six-teen-year-old girls *LOL*-ing, hoarding our trove of digital images: text and symbol. Uploading, but less loading up treasure—not to grind an axe—than laying the present moment, heavy and useless, ceremonially in the thick dust of itself. Our lives, bright relics.

THE GLITCH: POEM FOR 2016

When the world threw up its hands and wobble-tipped
into dysfunction: faction facing faction
posed in uncompromising opposition
and posting their insults over the abyss
—the logic binary, the tone *de trop*—
well, it all seemed an outsize version of the glitch
or gremlin in the works that harrowed us
and jammed the comms: Male wrath meets Female shame
and panic. Now too blindly passionate,
our words contract round one another's throat.

Who set the snares? Who wired so weirdly wrong
the circuits? The outrageous Patriarchs
sitting in state or—yes!—the one that stalks
up through your blighted childhood hectoring
and sowing fear might know. We don't. We watch
the displaced flee or freeze in alleyways.
Our righteous take their vigils to the streets—
homogenous, peremptory and too late,
their cry, re-echoed, one of disbelief:
who woke us to the bad dream of our life?

Who broke the loom and lobbed the first lout's stone
so that this mirror cracked from side to side
that we'd eyeballed, oblivious, so long

shocking us roughly into adulthood?
The year prolongs its asshole smash and grab
its wrecking spree—with us on separate coasts,
hunched round the narratives of all we've lost
like two spectators on apocalypse.
And, searching for where the blame lies in this matter,
we rifle bleakly through the microdata.

THE MAST

The steel stayed mast
high above sea level
is reached by a rough path
through yellow upland heath
and rock gravel.
The city lies beneath.

Though it could be any big town
raised above its past.
Sojourning on the coast,
a Brahmin might peer down
and form a fanciful list
of people here—each *himself*.

To the south are hills.
A barn. A ploughed-up field.
And under white heat shimmer,
an afternoon—where a Child
at the bend of a lane, pausing, feels
The Essential Summer.

Then behind the tracks
of a miniature railway line
and the kitchen backs
of terraces—close to what's known,
guided by blind feeling,
is that Kid grown . . .

Among the built sprawl
and glittering urban scree
are various other types.
And from the hilltops
the glazed God's-eye
of the transmitter sees them all.

In parks and back bars,
there is the Outsider
nursing his hurt. And indoors/
outdoors—everywhere here—there is the Mother
who jumps from self to other
like a stunt rider.

The city is low-rise,
small—and beyond white turbines
and old problematic spires
its centre turns
outward from folk's desires
and on their enterprise.

So, of various ranks,
each *striving*, each intent,
are imagined workers. In office blocks
near the docks
there is an Artist and a Merchant.
There are various guys in banks.

Or in well-designed spaces
down cobbled side streets,
where people stroke like pets
familiar devices,
there is, tallying debt
and also *striving*, the Graduate

who serves bespoke coffees,
smiling, to the fervent
sly undergraduate Student
from one or another school . . .
Look: each of them suffers.
The world is cruel.

I've lived so far
down in its machine
and painful source
I've seen not the woods—but trees
that this year
bloom to a Jurassic green

round the tract seen from
the old stayed radio mast.
And where—past
all this industry, and the lives
held in its eminent perspectives—
somewhere, also, is home.

Poems Conceived as
Dialogues between Two
Antagonistic Voices

FIRST DIALOGUE

Characters

The Scene is a restaurant in which the infant is crying, preceded by Woman's expedition there, with longueurs, bending, rustling, many minute and interminable activities, up close and out of focus.

WOMAN, IN RECEIPT

I moved from a world of air to one of earth.
Ash in my mouth. Dung on the high white table.
An endless cycle: milk and excrement,
as though I were a new bend in the gut
or part of the mouth, a fork propelling food,
a mode or means. A kind of vital function.

MAN, IMPATIENT

It's true the selflessness of women is extraordinary.

WOMAN, IN RECEIPT

Yes. Fuck off. You praise 'women' while you fail them
like drunks and statesmen. Look, her modest smile
and massive breasts, the gentle folded hands—
how easily she forms the room's calm heart . . .
Look, if some glass thing should topple from your desk
and I reach out my hands to break its fall
would you praise as momentous my reflexive reach?

MAN, IMPATIENT

I'm afraid, dear, I don't 'catch' you.

WOMAN, IN RECEIPT

I am the hands stretched out to break a fall.
I am the body startled out of sleep.
I am the straining ear, the watchful eye.
I'm the nerved body schooled in vigilance.
I am entirely conscious through all this.
I am in process. I am an active verb.

MAN, IMPATIENT

An active verb and now an activist?
You're conscious, so you're raising consciousness?
Give me a break, love. None of your cow-kind
will ever rouse themselves to re-define
the slavery that each wished on herself.
Tempted by sentiment, you take the plunge
then start up in the wreckage of your life
clutching some grievance you imagine new,
some ancient grievance, some antique complaint.

WOMAN, IN RECEIPT

I moved from a world of air: an arrow's path
speeding through space, my cool and ordered limbs
under control. Once in the height of summer
I caught an old, completely empty bus.
It travelled from the quiet, ripening fields
and stagnant ditches, up to the strange, hushed city
which seemed a place of marvellous planes and angles.
Just before lunchtime, all the streets were bare,
and sunlight struck the distant hospital.
Each wall contained—I thought—some brilliant drama.
Life was a place of space and mystery.

MAN, IMPATIENT

None of your herd, no, none of your low sort.
The bitch straining her leash to bite the pups . . .
Heaven preserve us, *mater dolorosa*,
what did you think was going to happen then?
You dream us up, freak out—and turn us loose
into the corridors of your resentment,
proving true after all the poet's words:
'They fuck you up, your mum and dad'.

[gleefully]

They fuck you up your mum and dad
They do not mean to but they do . . .

WOMAN, IN RECEIPT

[continuing]

Who in this mad arrangement *wouldn't* be
recalibrated by proximity?

*[to baby who, wait, is not, in fact, crying. 'Lovingly', spot-lit,
assuming the role with full theatrics to growing applause]*

But put me in your mouth, then, chew me up
on bony gums—and later when you sleep
digesting me alongside each new day,
well then I'll resume the story of myself
one hour at a time. Like sunsets speeded up,
or time-lapsed bloom and growth on forest floors
in some heritage thing by David Attenborough.
'Amazing that this most important work
should hardly require intelligence at all!' . . .
It's stranger, I think, you reckon me inert
by virtue of my not just walking off—
as though I wasn't a body on the wire,
or a hand held, open, over this open flame.

SECOND DIALOGUE

Characters

MAN, A FORMER ENVIRONMENTAL
ACTIVIST TURNED PR CONSULTANT
FOR LOGGING COMPANIES

VOICE, NEITHER MALE
NOR FEMALE, IMPERSONAL

The Scene is somewhere in Sumatra.

VOICE, NEITHER

The sky is blue. The fairybird is blue.
A great bird soars across the sky's blue dome,
its upturned bowl of brightest, brilliant blue
above the treeline and the canopy.
The canopy is closed: *Dipterocarpus*,
your timber-lumber, underneath whose crowns
smaller trees grow whose limbs form scaffolding
for creepers and climbers, herbs and smaller shrubs,
for the pitcher plant and the sun fern *Dipteris*
whose print is found in pre-historic fossils.

MAN, A FORMER

The dog barks, the cow moos, the sheep goes *baa*.
Man sizes up the cow and sheep
and clucking hen—and then puts them to use.
Look, answer this: if a tree falls in the forest
and no one's there to see it, will it burn?
Can it be stripped and pulped, packed and exported?
Does it make props and tiles? Or does it rot?

VOICE, NEITHER

The sky is blue. The distant sea is blue.
The moon's torque drags that salty wedge each day
up through the mangrove forests to the east,
where a little snail will climb its tree each morning
descending at evening—not to escape the tide
but through an evolved, coincidental rhythm.
The mangrove trees drop twigs and other litter
that crabs and fungi break to phosphorus-rich
mulch for the zooplankton; bottom-feeders
who feed, in turn, carnivorous fish and birds . . .

MAN, A FORMER

. . . who feed the bigger fish who then feed man,
the food-chain's top banana, cream of the crop

who pens in shrimp ponds and rips out raw gas.
Glory be his brain and spinal column,
his vertebrate strength and pelvis-threatening skull!
. . . You know, I see your point, when I was young
I thought that I would live . . . *reactively*;
cultivate plots, grow only what I need
but 'need' as a concept proves prone to expand.

VOICE, NEITHER

The sky is blue. The flycatcher is blue.
The king quail's breast is blue. The forest hosts
dark-handed gibbon, yellow-banded snake,
the snub-nosed monkey and the flying fox
which scents, at range, the lowland fruit and blossom
crash-landing into trees to feed on nectar.
The trees grow buttresses. Some hollow limbs
house porcupines and rats whose pungent waste
is milled by the little creatures in the soil
then tilled back to the red loam of the earth.

MAN, A FORMER

When I was young I thought the life I'd lead
would be passionate, nomadic, self-contained
with my nine bean rows and hives of buzzy bees . . .

I'd keep a few goats, use only what I need
—but oh how the boundaries of sufficiency
shift ever outwards. That's a fact of life.
Nests must be feathered, little mouths need fed.
And from such seeds do corporations grow.

VOICE, NEITHER

Here every kind of crawling rustling species,
from stinkhorn fungus to the giant flower,
jostles in constant restless composition
but the tree and its mast is root and branch of all.
The tree in its cycle is gregarious
so isopod crustaceans crowd in root-tips
and convex leaves shield colonies of ants.

MAN, A FORMER

So pitcher plants lure insects to their lips
to drown them; larvae browse over their corpses.
The hookworm and mosquito breed like this.
The forest hosts the opportunist killer
as the fig-tree hosts fig-wasp and parasite.
When man clears the trees he makes his destiny
along with the timber-yards and paper-mills,
and the scorch on the mountain is his signature.

VOICE, NEITHER

The sky is blue. The endless sky is blue.

MAN, A FORMER

The smoke hung above the chimney stacks is blue.

VOICE, NEITHER

The glinting fly and darting bird are blue.

MAN, A FORMER

The ink on my ledger's bottom line is blue.

THIRD DIALOGUE

Characters

MOTHER OF OLDER CHILD, IMPLODED

THE AWESOME VOICE OF THE INTERNET

The Scene is everywhere/nowhere.

MOTHER, IMPLODED

First it is frightening, then one grows strangely numb
like tramping lost for miles, through falling snow
squinting at each new bend for signs of home.
Here by some frozen junction box or stump
I can make out the margins of the town:
it's open and glittering like a jewellery box.
It's glittering. Bright. Unreachably far.

AWESOME VOICE

There are no margins and there is no centre;
only the loop, the circuit or the synapse
the nerve—connected, branched—through eye to hand
. . . and all of our devices. Answer this:

if one of your lonesome trees falls in the forest
and no one's there to photograph, record
and post the proof—does that tree make a sound?
No, and there is no such outsider forest,
Each tree's accounted for, and so are you.

MOTHER, IMPLODED

First it is all miraculously new:
a hospital's white, ringing corridor
that telescopes in front with each new step . . .
Ask me again how I got mislaid here,
down the white maze of thoughts—intent, shut in,
until it seems I *am* the corridor:
the wall that bounces back the baby's cry;
the space pressed round by hot contingencies;
and everything immediate—such voices!—
while, feebler and feebler, mine dies in my throat.

AWESOME VOICE

There is no such mute, abysmal inwardness,
Lady, come down from your barrack room or cell
and look about you: everything is surface;
the surface is what's there, and nothing can
exist except what's there—*Hello? Capisce?*

And on this bright and level playing field,
well, now is a time when voices can be heard!
The disenfranchised and the overlooked,
empowered and dragged from history's dismal blackness
to rest in daylight. In. The. Light. Of. Day.

MOTHER, IMPLODED

The day split open and I went to pieces:
a piece of me in the car or by the door,
a dozen 'me's for various obligations
like Michael Keaton in—what *was* that film?
And the child's demands, Christ, those I could fathom,
but all these others? Updates. High alerts
the BUZZ BUZZ BUZZ of following information
as each Messiah, on his separate mount,
heralds aloud the Age of Interruption.
No wonder I went scattering over the day
like this tissue shredded—see here—in my hands.
Look, I don't feel like talking about this anymore.

AWESOME VOICE

Not interruption, love, but participation.
The *Force Majeure* of the collective will
—Immediate! Connected! Validated!—

shaping its truths the way, well, hands shape clay.
We have no record of your great distress
here in the filtered stream or data set,
our archive of the *known*—and no lone tree
that's fruiting or swaying in its *jouissance*.
And while I'm the Bright, White Spirit of the Age,
you, if you will, are just some sagging *hausfrau*,
your gut a bag of fat, LOL, in your lap—
I'm sorry: redact. Delete. Report abuse.

MOTHER, IMPLODED

My mother left me in the hospital
once when I was ill at two or three
and nothing since then has really been the same.
I must have lain short-breathed and saucer-eyed
swallowing up the darkness for an age
until it settled at my very core.
It's the reason I'm a little like the girl
who runs in front of the fireworks and the band
twirling the coloured batons—in her mind.

Imagine! Such effort just to stand stock still!
But the world and its images are so relentless,
its speed and movement—right, I'll sit down now
and take from this shouting match some liberty.

'August 30th 2013' refers to Heaney's 'Elegy' for Robert Lowell, from *Fieldwork*, which contains the line 'The way we're living, / timorous or bold, / will have been our life'. Heaney wrote of John Ashbery in 1985, '. . . his poetry is a centrally-heated daydream. And it's also sorrowful, it knows that it's inadequate'.

'Malone Hoard' was written for the exhibition '26 Treasures' at the Ulster Museum, October 2011. The Malone Hoard consists of 16 porcellanite axeheads discovered at Danesfort House on the Malone Road, Belfast. Poems written in response to these exhibits were to be 62 words long. The axeheads look like iPhone 3s.

'Ode to Moy Park' was written for *The Vacuum Newspaper* for the 'Laureate of Business', Keith O'Keefe.

Lines at the end of 'First Dialogue', 'Amazing . . .' paraphrase comments in *The Child, the Family and the Outside World* by D. M. Winnicott. 'The Second Dialogue' was written in response to an article by George Monbiot about former Greenpeace activist Patrick Moore, published in the *Guardian*'s blog, December 2010. All further details are from a study, *The Ecology of Sumatra*, by Tony Whitten.

৯৯

Acknowledgements are due to the following publications: *Causeway*, *Edinburgh Review*, *Granta*, *The Lifeboat*, *Kathleen Jamie: Essays and Poems on her Work*, *Poetry Ireland*, *Poetry London*, *Poetry Review*, and *THE SHOp*.

৯৯

To my large, endlessly supportive family, at their different removes and of different generations, thank you. Profound thanks also to Robin Robertson.